Hidden Hazards of Quilting

the
Hidden Hazards
of Quilting

Cathy Watts

Copyright © 1996 by Cathy Watts

No part of this book may be reproduced or transmitted in any form by any means, electronic or mechanical, including photocopying and recording, or by any information storage or retrieval system without prior written permission from the author, except for brief passages quoted in a review.

Canadian Cataloguing in Publication Data

    Watts, Cathy, 1948–

    The hidden hazards of quilting

    Includes bibliographical references and index.
    ISBN 0–9699999–0–9

    1. Quilting - Physiological aspects. 2. Overuse injuries - Prevention. I. Title.

    TT835.W37 1996   746.46   C95–920240–4

Jacket design by Aaron Leighton and Janine Vangool
Cover and interior illustrations by Aaron Leighton
Photography by AK Photos
Editing, page layout and design by Pagewood Publishing Services, Saskatoon
Printed and bound in Canada
Published by Physio-Diversity

Orders and inquiries to: **Physio-Diversity**
    1136 Temperance Street
    Saskatoon, Saskatchewan
    Canada S7N 0N8
    Tel: (306) 664-3908

Author's Note: Although most quilters are female, there are some men who quilt. The pronoun "she" is used exclusively throughout this book, with apologies to the male reader.

Acknowledgements: Richard Bourassa, Sharon Kingston, Barb Dawson, and the Saskatoon Quilters' Guild; Wanda Bristol, who modelled for the photographs, and Elaine Sedgman, who started it all.

To my husband and children for their support, encouragement and sense of humour.

Contents

Preface   11

1   **Quilting Is Hazardous to Your Health**   13
      Is Quilting a Sedentary Activity or an Olympic Event?

2   **Sitting Matters**   19
      Poor Sitting Posture
      What Does a Good Sitting Posture Look Like?
      How to Sit Comfortably
      Things to Remember About Sitting

3   **What Has Your Size Got to Do with Quilting?**   27
      Measuring Yourself
      Key Anthropometric Dimensions for Chair Design

4   **What You Should Know About Chairs**   31
      Important Features of Your Chair
      How to Buy a New Chair or Evaluate Your Current Chair
      How to Adapt Your Chair
      Tips on Sitting Comfortably
      Troubleshooting Chart for Chairs

5   **Putting Chair and Table Together**   43
      Designing or Reading in a Sitting Position
      Working at the Sewing Machine in a Sitting Position
      Using a Quilting Frame

Contents

5 Putting Chair and Table Together cont.
Tips on Combining Your Chair and Work Surface
Troubleshooting Chart for Height of Work Surface

6 Standing Can Be a Pain   51
How to Stand Correctly
Making the Most of Standing
Work Table Height When Standing
Shoes
Tips on Standing Comfortably

7 Designing Your Work Station   59
Organizing Your Space
Organizing the Sequence of Your Work
Tips on Organizing Your Work

8 Choosing Your Tools   65
Tips on Choosing Tools

9 Other Health Hazards   69
Circulatory Problems
Repetitive Strain Injuries
    How Do Repetitive Strain Injuries Occur?
    Where Does the Injury Occur?
    Recognising Repetitive Strain Injuries
    Tips on Preventing Repetitive Strain Injuries

10 Going to a Quilting Workshop   77
Creative Comfort at the Workshop
Getting to and from the Workshop
Tips on Lifting Heavy Loads

Contents 9

11 Exercises and Stretches to Make You Feel Great   85
    When to Exercise
    How to Exercise
    The Exercises
        Sitting
        Standing
        Lying

Equipment List   119
    Back Supports
    Chairs
    Lighting
    Luggage Carts
    Portable Work Surfaces

References   121

Index   122

Author's Note   126

Order Form   127

Preface

I had no sooner begun my passionate journey into the world of quilting when I discovered an unwelcome companion—pain. Being a physiotherapist, I was acutely aware of the problems of poor posture when performing a repetitive or prolonged task. Fellow quilters had also warned me that despite the creative enjoyment of this leisure-time pursuit, there come with it a lot of physical ailments—some of them serious enough to prevent the quilter from continuing to quilt. I also became aware that the equipment quilters use is not always suited to the individual.

The time has come to promote wellness for quilters by providing information they can use to make themselves as comfortable as possible. The intent of this book is to show readers how to adapt what they currently own and have become accustomed to using to enhance their comfort and productivity. If readers are in the market for new pieces of equipment this book will also help them to understand the important features that are necessary to ensure good posture and fit. Adapting to situations away from the comforts of the home set-up at workshops or classes, as well as exercises for warming up and stretches during the quilting process, are included.

This publication is intended to help the quilter offset the adverse effects of prolonged sitting and allow the quilter many years of happy, productive, and painfree quilting.

Happy Quilting!

Quilting is an addiction for me. Even in the middle of completing an addition one summer I had to unpack my sewing equipment and work on a quilting project. It has a calming effect on me.

                                              Linda Landine

1

Quilting Is Hazardous to Your Health

The aim of this book is to explain how you can absorb yourself in your passion without placing undue strain on your body. Quilting is by nature a repetitive activity. Besides the usual complaint of stabbed fingers, fellow quilters also report stiff necks, tender and aching muscles, sore backs, numbness in the legs, and varicose veins. Quite simply, if you spend hours in poor postures, totally absorbed by the creative process, using poorly designed equipment, you run the risk of hurting yourself.

In the normal process of getting older, posture changes. For women in particular there is a tendency for an increased curve in the upper back. The scourge of osteoporosis, which affects one in four women over the age of

---

I can't understand it. I've only been quilting for five hours!

sixty, emphasizes this change. Poor posture may aggravate the pain associated with curvature of the spine and may lead to further deformity. It is particularly important for quilters, who engage in repetitive tasks, to pay attention to their posture to offset the natural process of aging.

As we grow older, the wear and tear on our bodies becomes more noticeable. Years of improper sitting or standing cause excessive wear and premature aging of the joints. Over the long term, the consequences of poor posture can be as harmful as the effects of an injury. To help prevent injury to your joints over time, good posture is essential, and it is important for you to choose equipment that will promote good posture during the long absorbing hours you spend at your craft.

With the growing interest in quilting, there are many new products that promise to make the quilter's life more comfortable. You need to evaluate each of these products carefully. No matter what they promise, be aware that some of them are useless, some can be adapted to your individual needs, and others are essential. If you understand the basics of good posture and know how to adapt equipment to your individual size and situation, you will be able to purchase equipment that will work well for you and you will avoid wasting money. (Money that could have been spent on more fabric!)

Making a quilt gives me confidence in what creativity I have. It helps me go forward from there.

Catherine Rostron

I like Amish quilts the best because of their brilliant colours. I made one that I have hanging in the kitchen. Every morning I look at it while I'm having breakfast and it gives me a great deal of pleasure.

Shirley Collins

I wonder if this is essential?

Is Quilting a Sedentary Activity or an Olympic Event?

Let's face it, you do not move around much when you quilt, and if all you did was quilt all day, you would not be very fit. If you are not fit, your muscles lose strength, which then makes moving around more difficult. If you do not move around much, circulation and the digestive processes deteriorate. Although this deterioration may not be serious enough to stop you doing the things you want to do, it can make you susceptible to other diseases with more serious consequences. The good news is that there are things you can do to offset the essentially sedentary nature of the task.

Although you do not expend much energy when you quilt, the stress put on joints and muscles by small repetitive tasks can rival the stress put on the body by more intensely physical activities. Many quilters have stories about serious back problems, headaches, and pain in muscles or tendons due to quilting. Even when you are sitting still, the muscles of your back and neck are working to keep you sitting up straight and the small muscles of your hands and wrists are involved in fine repetitive work that can be as stressful for these muscles as the larger muscle work involved in a major athletic competition. Sometimes the pain that results from quilting activities can be serious enough to severely limit your pleasure in the craft and the amount of time you are able to spend pursuing this activity.

So how can something that is so much fun and that provides so many hours of passionate creativity be so bad for you? If you are reading this book, there is no way you are going to quit an activity

---

Quilting allows me to express my feelings.

Marg Cloake

you enjoy so much. What you need to do, then, is to adapt your chair, the set-up of your sewing space, and your other quilting equipment to ensure that you can quilt in a healthy and comfortable manner. Just what this arrangement will be will differ slightly from individual to individual. The general tips in this book will help you choose the best arrangement for you. As you will see, it is also important that you balance quilting activities with physical exercises designed to counteract the effects of prolonged sitting and working at repetitive tasks.

Discomfort and fatigue have an effect on performance and pleasure. In addition, poor posture, poorly designed equipment, and factors such as inadequate lighting, noise level, and general environmental discomfort all reduce the level of enjoyment you can get from quilting. Quilters frequently spend hours planning the next quilt. Taking time now to learn how to structure your quilting activities will lead to years of comfort and productivity in the future.

I love the ability to be creative and to create a work of art from all kinds of fabrics that by themselves don't express anything.

Grace Whittington

2

Sitting Matters

Sitting for a long time is probably the unhealthiest posture there is for the human body, and prolonged sitting with poor posture over time is a major cause of lower back pain. Sitting increases pressure on the discs, causes stress on the posterior wall of the discs and on the ligaments in the lower back, decreases blood flow in the legs, reduces respiratory and digestive functions, and increases muscle fatigue in the neck and back.

Sitting causes stress on the posterior wall of the discs and ligaments in the lower back.

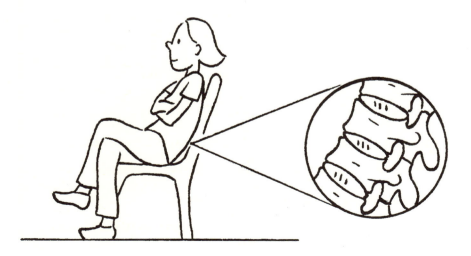

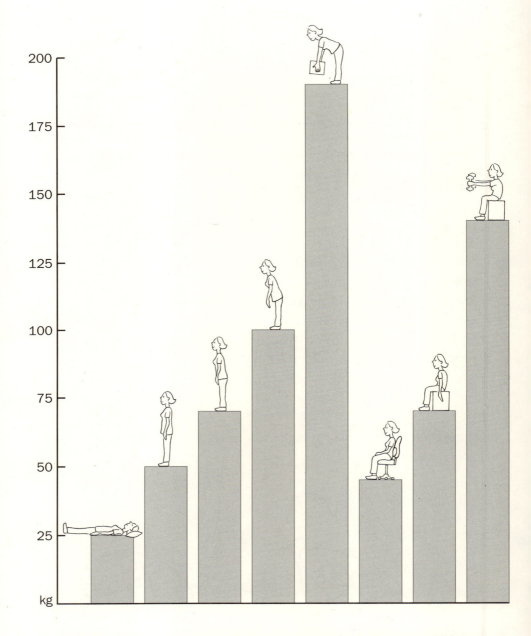

This graph illustrates the **relative pressure within the third lumbar disc** in various positions. Pressure is least while lying down and greatest when lifting an object with back bent and knees straight.

(Data used with permission: Alf Nachamson M.D.)

Studies have been done on the amount of pressure in the discs in the lower back in various postures. The positions that produce the highest pressure are standing or sitting with the trunk leaning forward. These are common postures in many activities that we do during the day but particularly in quilting positions. Pressure in the discs produces abnormal changes in disc shape, a loss of flexibility in the spine, and increased risk of injury or pain.

Quilters who spend great portions of their day in the workplace as office workers or in jobs that require continuous sitting are particularly vulnerable to the risks of injury or discomfort from prolonged sitting.

Poor Sitting Posture

Sitting may appear to be a position that requires less effort than more obviously strenuous tasks such as gardening, but the effort of sitting up straight for a long time can cause a great deal of discomfort if your body is not adequately supported. When you sit still, your muscles contract and less blood flows to them. With reduced circulation, the muscles become fatigued and are then susceptible to injury if the activity continues. A vicious circle of pain, spasm, and decreased circulation develops.

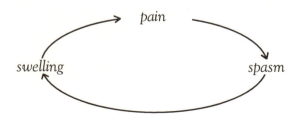

Prolonged sitting without proper support and without interruptions of activity can lead to pooling of blood in the legs, which

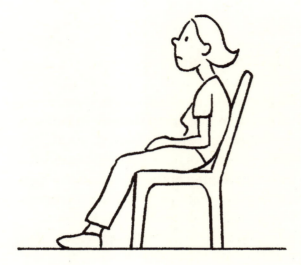

In a slumped position, it takes energy to hold your head upright.

can cause swollen ankles. More serious problems such as blood clots can also occur in people who are susceptible to circulatory problems. Poor circulation generally causes muscles to get tired sooner, which can lead to a general sense of fatigue by the end of the day. Poorly fitting chairs that put pressure on the underside of the thigh can reduce circulation and further aggravate the situation.

If you are in the habit of quilting on a horizontal surface in front of you, you will find that you need to tilt your head forward so you can see your work. When you do this, you use the muscles in your upper back and neck to keep your head from falling forward. If you do not have adequate back support, you will tend to compensate for the energy it takes to keep your head up by sitting in a slumped posture.

It takes a great deal of energy to sit in a rounded position while holding up your head to see what you are doing. In this position, the muscles of your trunk must work very hard to hold your body erect so that your hands are free to move. Sitting in a slumped position causes your abdominal muscles to become slack, which contributes to increased disc pressure in your spine. As well, this position constricts the lungs and digestive system.

What Does a Good Sitting Posture Look Like?

While you are reading this page make sure that your bottom is well back in your chair and that your lower back and the area in between your shoulder blades are both supported by the back of your chair. With your head centred and your eyes looking straight ahead, gently bring your chin back in what is known as the "chin tuck." This is usually a balanced position. Take a slow deep breath being conscious of the air moving in and out as your chest moves up and down.

Now relax your head letting your chin protrude forward. You will also experience a rounding of your shoulders in the upper back. If you let yourself relax further, the area between your shoulder blades will start to move forward and become more rounded. At this point you may also feel your rib cage moving down towards your abdomen. Take another slow deep breath. You may feel that this breath is more restricted and is more focused in the abdominal area. As you let your back round, the abdominal muscles become slack and lower the pressure in the abdominal area. As the muscle tone decreases in

A good sitting posture.

the abdomen, there will be a corresponding increase in the pressure on the discs in the spine.

If you were to remain sitting in this posture, you would soon notice that your lower back was also becoming rounded. If you let your bottom slide forward in your chair a few centimetres, you would soon be sitting in a very poor posture indeed. Sitting in this position for an extended period of time would produce neck and shoulder pain, as well as pain in your lower back.

How to Sit Comfortably

Our bodies are constantly working against gravity to remain erect, and sitting is basically an unstable position. Without the support of a good chair, the muscles of the neck and back tire quickly. The key to comfort in sitting is to provide good support to prevent poor posture and to find an appropriate balance between sedentary activity and movement. A good sitting posture varies from individual to individual, depending on body shape and size, habitual behaviour, and personal preference. Few of us have perfect posture. The effects of time may have produced changes that are now difficult to correct. Given these imperfections, it is important to work towards the ideal to prevent further changes. Even a good sitting posture that is maintained for an extended period can be uncomfortable, which is why it is important to change positions regularly and to intersperse periods of sitting with other activities.

I've spent as much on physiotherapy as on quilting. It's a hazard.

Betty Sanguin

Things to Remember About Sitting

It is not only important to sit properly, it is also important to change your position often when sitting. There are a number of reasons for this, including:
- To take pressure off the bones in your seat to prevent or reduce swelling, discomfort, and pain.
- To prevent buildup of temperature and humidity.
- To prevent trunk, shoulders, and neck from becoming fatigued.
- To promote movement of the discs in your spine for better health.
- To promote circulation in your lower legs.

In addition, it is important to alternate sitting with another activity every forty-five to sixty minutes. Changing positions regularly and having a balance between activities is necessary for complete comfort and promotion of overall well-being.

I do a lot of dreaming when I'm quilting. Usually it's about the next quilt I want to do, so I quilt faster and faster to get onto the next one!

Ruth Sirota

3

What Has Your Size Got to Do with Quilting?

There is no such person as an "average person." We all come in different sizes and shapes, and we all have different preferences. Despite this, you will find many products for quilters that are specifically designed for this fictitious "average person." If you purchase equipment with a variety of adjustable features, you can use the information in this book to make the item more functional and comfortable for your own individual situation.

It is important to customize your whole system to your body shape and preferences. This includes your chair, table, lighting,

---

There is no such thing as an average person.

sewing worksite, and quilting frame. In many cases, the changes required can be done inexpensively with some creative adaptations to your present equipment; if you are currently in the market for a new piece of equipment, the information in the chart will help you to make a purchase that will enhance your comfort for the rest of your quilting life.

Measuring Yourself

First of all you need to know what size you are. The diagram and chart will help you with the body measurements you need to know to determine the proper heights and distances that will be comfortable for you. You will also be able to determine what percentile of the total population you fit into—that is to say, what percentage of the total population shares your body shape and size. For example, if you are in the fifth percentile in some areas (for example, thigh

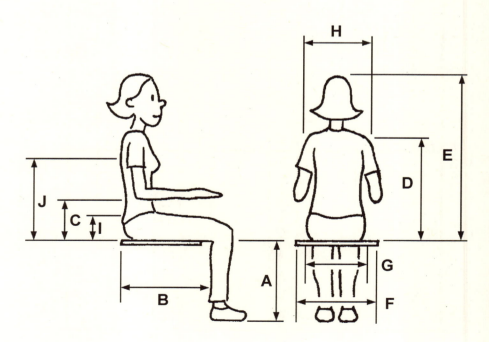

Key Anthropometric Dimensions for Chair Design

Measurement	Men				Women				Your Measurements	
	5th percentile		95th percentile		5th percentile		95th percentile			
	cm	in	cm	in	cm	in	cm	in	cm	in
A Knee to Floor	39.5	15.5	49	19.3	35.5	14	44.5	17.5		
B Thigh Length	44	17.3	55	21.6	43.5	17	53	20.9		
C Elbow Rest Height	19.5	7.7	29.5	11.6	18.5	7.3	28	11		
D Shoulder Height	54	21.3	64.5	25.4	50.5	19.9	61	24		
E Sitting Height	80.3	31.6	93	36.6	75.2	29.6	88.1	34.7		
F Elbow to Elbow Width	34.8	13.7	50.5	19.9	31.2	12.3	49	19.3		
G Hip Width	31	12.2	40.5	15.9	31	12.2	43.5	17.1		
H Shoulder Width	43.2	17	48.3	19	33	13	48.3	19		
I Seat to Lower Back Height	19.5	7.7	28.5	11.2	19.5	7.7	26.5	10.4		
J Scapular Height	40.5	15.9	48	18.9	38	15	45	17.7		

Adapted from Ergonomics, Work, and Health by S. Pheasant. Copyright © 1991 by S. Pheasant. Used with permission of Macmillan Press, and Human Dimension and Interior Space by Julius Panero and Martin Zelnik. Copyright © 1979 by Julius Panero and Martin Zelnik. Used with permission of Whitney Library of Design, an imprint of Watson-Guptill Publications.

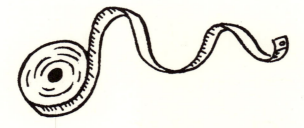

length) you likely have already found it difficult to find a chair that is short enough to fit you. You will need to have a buddy to help you with these measurements. The only other equipment you require is a measuring tape and a firm surface to sit on.

I love colours. Selecting a variety of fabrics for a quilt and watching the design emerge is the part of the creative process I really enjoy.

Barb Dawson

4

What You Should Know About Chairs

The first piece of equipment you need to evaluate is your chair. A good chair is comfortable, gives support, and allows changes in body position. What is comfortable depends on the individual, how the chair is used, and how long the chair is used.

When you sit, you feel pressure through the bones in your bottom. For the person with a slight frame and very little padding, this can be quite uncomfortable if the chair seat is hard and flat. There is a bursa or sac that provides cushioning between the bone and the surrounding tissue. Prolonged localized pressure may irritate this sac, causing local pain as well as irritating the surrounding structures. For the person with more generous padding, the body weight is distributed over a larger area and such localized irritation is less likely to be a problem.

If your chair is not wide enough, you may feel pressure along the sides of your thighs near your hip bones. Squeezing into a chair that is too narrow will cause your hips to rotate, which will then

---

Quilting has filled an empty space for me.
Ruth Sirota

lead to other problems that will cause discomfort. For the woman with large breasts, there is a tendency to lean forward—so it is particularly important to make sure the pelvis and lower back are well supported to counteract this tendency. Contrary to what many of us have been taught, it is neither comfortable nor practical to sit up straight and not slump in a chair that has a high vertical backrest. Studies show that there is a significant decrease in muscle activity, and therefore stress, when the back is slightly inclined backwards to stabilize the trunk.

Any chair can be comfortable for a short time. For extended periods of sitting (more than one hour), which is the norm in quilting activities, it is important to consider several features that will promote your comfort and well-being.

Important Features of Your Chair

Seat Depth and Surface
- The seat should not press the undersides of your thighs.
- The front edge of the seat should curve downwards.
- The fabric on the seat should not slip and should "breathe." Avoid stiff, non-stretch fabrics such as canvas or plastic.
- A contoured seat will reduce the pressure points on your bottom that occur with a hard flat seat, allowing you to sit longer without discomfort.
- Excessive contour puts pressure on your hips and tends to roll your legs inwards.

Seat Height
- When your bottom is firmly against the back of your chair, your feet should be flat on the floor.

Height, Tilt (Angle), and Design of Backrest
- The backrest should support your lower back by following the contour of your spine and allowing room for your buttocks.

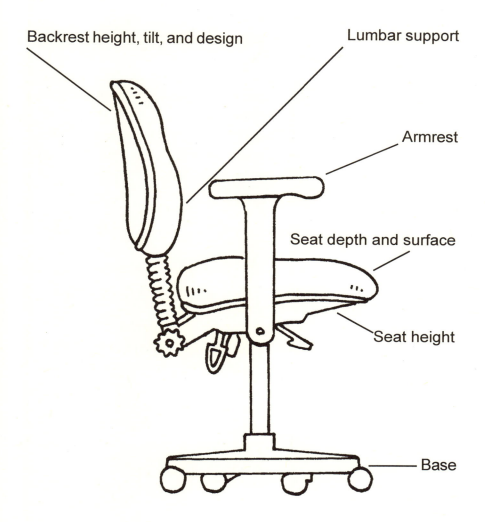

Important features of a chair.

- A backwards tilt of approximately 15 degrees is desirable. If the back of your chair does not lean back, you can use a footrest to achieve a similar effect.
- The backrest should be flat from side to side or only slightly hollowed so that your shoulders and shoulder blades are not pushed forward.
- The backrest should not put pressure on the outer part of your shoulder blades and shoulders.
- The backrest should come up to just below the lower angle of your shoulder blades; a high vertical backrest, such as is sometimes found on dining room chairs, is not desirable.

Lumbar Support

- Place a lumbar roll in the small of your back at the level of your beltline.
- Whether you are using a rolled-up towel or a commercial product, the diameter of the lumbar roll should not exceed 4 cm (1.5 in) when it is compressed.
- You may find the lumbar support uncomfortable for the first few days as your back will not be used to the new position, but continued use will improve your lower back posture.

Armrests

- If your forearms are not supported, they will pull down on the muscles in your neck and shoulders causing stiffness and soreness.
- The weight of your forearms if they are not supported tends to pull your upper body forward and downward away from the backrest of your chair. The resulting slumped posture adversely affects the position of your head and neck, causing you to stick your head out forward.
- If your forearms are supported, you take some of the pressure off your bottom.
- The armrests should be low enough that you can rest your arms on them without them elevating your shoulders.

- The armrests should also be low enough that you can pull the chair under the table so you can hold your back straight and sit with your stomach held gently against the front of the work surface.

Chair Base
- The chair must be stable—five legs are a good idea but not essential.
- A swivel mechanism that allows you to turn in the chair without rotating your body is desirable but not essential.

How to Buy a New Chair or Evaluate Your Current Chair

Seat Depth and Surface
Sit in the chair so that you are well back in it. You should have no sense of slipping forward; you must feel stable. You should have room for four fingers between the front edge of the chair and the back of your knees. Women often find chair seats are too deep because women tend to be shorter than the "average man" for whom some chairs are made. Make sure the chair accommodates your hips so that there is no pressure along the sides of your thighs.

Seat Height
Always wear flat-soled shoes. As you sit in the chair, your feet should be firmly on the floor with your weight distributed evenly over the whole foot—not just the toes. You can use a footrest to adjust the height of your chair. If you don't own a footrest, you can make one from books or an old telephone book wrapped in duct tape.

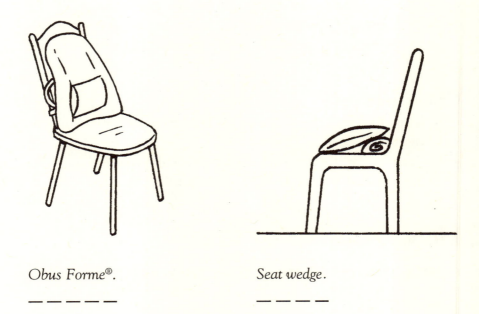

Obus Forme®. *Seat wedge.*

Height, Tilt (Angle), and Design of Backrest

The backrest should come up to your shoulder blades. If it is too high it can force your upper back forward. It is better to buy a chair with a backrest that is too low rather than too high. You should be able to tilt the chair back 110 to 120 degrees (that is, at least 15 degrees past a 90-degree angle and preferably a little more). If your chair back does not move, you can use a footrest from time to time to vary the angle at which you are sitting.

Adjust the backrest to support the hollow in your lower back. If there is a lumbar roll, adjust it to the height where you would wear a belt. If the backrest is not adjustable and provides little support, you can purchase a back insert such as an Obus Forme® (see equipment list) or similar product. A seat wedge will help tip the pelvis forward to restore the lumbar curve. You can improvise your own seat wedge by rolling a towel to a diameter of 5 cm (2–3 in) and placing it under the back of the seat cushion. A type of back support called the Nada-Chair® can also be used to support the lower back.

What You Should Know About Chairs 37

Nada-Chair®.

— — — —

Because straps go around the knees and back, you must take it off if you wish to stand up. It is useful for prolonged sitting but is inconvenient if you need to get up frequently.

Armrests

Relax your arms by your side and bend your elbows to a 90-degree angle. The armrests should support your forearms at this height. If the armrests are not the right height, it is better to have them too low rather than too high. If they are too high they will force your shoulders upwards. If they are too low you can always find ways to raise them. The armrests should be positioned so that they are close to your body.

Price

Price is not always a guiding factor; an expensive chair can be uncomfortable for you.

Controls
The controls to adjust the chair should work well and be easy to use.

Store Policy
The store should allow you to try the chair out at home for a day to see if it suits you. If it is impractical to try the chair out at home, spend at least ten to fifteen minutes sitting in it in the store.

The Most Important Question
The most important question you can ask is: does the chair feel comfortable for you?

How to Adapt Your Chair

Depending on your size and the chairs that are available to you, it may not be possible for you to find the perfect chair. Even if you do find a chair that is a good fit, you may have to share it with others who will need to be able to customize it to their particular size. Look around your living space and try several chairs to find the one that is closest to a good fit for you. Then look at the chart at the end of this chapter to find ways of adapting your chosen chair to your particular requirements.

I get a backache when I sew too much—like six hours at a stretch. Maybe I'm not sitting right.

Marg Cloake

Tips on Sitting Comfortably

- Have good back support.
- Have good foot support.
- Vary your sitting position by adjusting the backward tilt of the chair or by using a footrest periodically.
- Align your head vertically with your spine, tucking your chin in.
- Distribute your weight evenly over the chair seat.
- Keep your shoulders low and relaxed.
- Keep your elbows tucked in and supported if at all possible.
- Keep your wrists straight and aligned with your forearms.
- Pull your chair under the table so that your stomach is touching the work surface.
- Do not sit for more than forty-five minutes at a time.

Situation	What Happens?	Leads To	Possible Correction
1 Seat too high	• gives no support for feet (dangling legs) • puts pressure on back of legs • causes buttocks to slide forward so feet can touch the ground • destabilizes body as you perch on the edge of your chair	• slumped posture • whole body tiredness	• lower seat if adjustable • use footrest to support feet
2 Seat too low	• puts pressure on internal organs • disrupts blood circulation to lower legs • puts too much pressure on buttocks	• legs swell • burning sensation in buttocks	• raise chair with platform
3 Seat too deep	• puts pressure behind knees • either gives no support for back (forward position) or gives poor support for lower back (if you lean back in a flexed position)	• slumped posture • tired muscles in back	• decrease depth with Obus Forme® cushion or lumbar support • use Nada-Chair®
4 Slippery upholstery	• causes you to slide forward	• slumped posture • feeling of instability in chair	• cover upholstery with nonslip fabric • wear clothes that provide more friction • use a piece of antislip mat on top of chair and place small nonslip cushion on top

	Situation	What Happens?	Leads To	Possible Correction
5	Soft upholstery or inappropriate contouring	• puts pressure on buttocks	• slumped posture • inability to sit for any length of time	• use a denser cushion • use a seat system from Obus Forme® or similar product
6	Chair back too vertical	• causes you to move buttocks forward to get support for back and to stabilize yourself in the chair	• slumped posture	• choose a different chair
7	Chair back too low	• causes you to move buttocks forward to get more support for your back	• slumped posture	• choose a different chair • use a back support such as Obus Forme® if the chair back is high enough to hold it in position
8	Rigid back support leans backwards more than 10 degrees	• gives no support for back, causing you to pull away from chair back and lean forward	• slumped posture	• choose a different chair • use a cushion and lumbar support (if this reduces the seat depth too much, choose a different chair) • use a Nada-Chair®

Troubleshooting Chart for Chairs

The most sentimental quilt I've ever made was for a very special baby girl. It was designed to reflect the environment at the cottage at the lake. Besides keeping her warm, it represents a happy place that I hope she'll learn to love and be part of.

Shirley Collins

5

Putting Chair and Table Together

Once you have selected your chair, it is time to consider your work surface. The height of the work surface is as important to your general posture and well-being as the size and shape of your chair. The ideal height varies depending on the task and whether you are standing or sitting. When you are quilting, you need to be able to move your hands and see what you are doing at the same time. The height of the work surface will be a compromise between the optimum height for your arms and the optimum position of your head and body. A combination that allows you to keep your chin tucked in as you work minimizes pain and discomfort in the upper back and neck. Your arms will be more comfortable if they can be supported in a relaxed position that does not raise your shoulders.

Designing or Reading in a Sitting Position

The height of the work surface should be about the height of your elbows when you are sitting in your chair with your arms hanging straight down by your sides. (This is measurement A plus measurement C on the chart in chapter 3.)

A sloping surface improves neck posture.

When you are designing a quilt or reading, a sloping work surface brings the work to the eye instead of you having to bring your eye to the work. You can use a commercial product such as a drafting board, but if you understand what you need, you can also adapt your existing work surface. You can create a sloping surface by raising the back legs of your work table with small blocks or books. A slope of 15 degrees is adequate when you are writing or using your hands for another activity. A greater slope is not desirable because it does not give you enough support for your arms. You will need a rim along the lower edge of a sloping work surface to prevent objects from slipping off. Remember to allow enough room to pull your legs under the table, as well as room to stretch your legs out straight.

Quilting can be as solitary or as social as you want it to be.   — Sandy Parsons

Working at the Sewing Machine in a Sitting Position

Sewing at the machine requires the combined use of eyes, hands, and arms. For this type of work, the work surface of the sewing machine should be 10 to 30 cm (4–12 in) below eye height. You can raise the height of your sewing machine by placing a small block under the legs of your sewing table or by placing a small block of wood under the edge of the sewing machine.

Sometimes it is just not possible to adjust the height of the work surface you are using. For example, if you are sewing on Grandmother's antique dining room table cutting the legs down a few centimetres is not an option; however, there are several other adaptations you can make when preparing your work environment for comfort if you consider the total package of chair and work surface.

Raising chair to fit high table.

Machine tilted to improve view.

If your work surface is too high and cannot be lowered, you can raise your chair instead by placing it on a platform that supports your chair and feet. One problem with raising your chair to meet your table is that there may not be room for your legs under the table. It may take some experimenting to find the ideal combination. As it is usually easier to adjust the height of a chair than a table, always consider adjustments to the chair first.

To keep your back in symmetrical alignment while using your machine, align the needle of the machine directly in front of you. If you tilt the sewing machine forward so that the needle is 5 cm (2–3 in) higher than normal, you will get a better view of your work without having to hunch over to see it. Keep your arms close to your body with your hands resting on the "deck" of the sewing machine. Armrests on your chair can provide elbow support, but make sure your shoulders are not elevated and remain relaxed. Place the pedal for the sewing machine directly in front of you so you do not have to twist your hips to reach it.

Putting Chair and Table Together 47

Using a Quilting Frame

A frame that tilts is best—that way you can easily adjust your work to a height that is comfortable for you. The plastic floor frames that snap together are an example of a product that is designed for the "average quilter." Without adjustment this kind of frame is unlikely to fit your needs; however, if you know what the optimal height is for your size (see the chart in chapter 3), you can easily adapt the frame to your personal requirements.

You can build the frame up to the proper height with blocks or books. It is the degree of tilt, however, that is particularly important. It should be tilted towards you so that you do not have to poke your chin and head forward to see what you are doing. If the tilt of the frame cannot be adjusted, you can still increase or decrease it by putting extra blocks or books under the back legs. Be aware that any frame that is not adjustable in height or tilt will likely require some adaptation in order to promote your own individual comfort.

When you quilt in a frame or hoop on your lap, your work should be 0 to 15 cm (0–6 in) above elbow height. Ideally, your elbows should be supported, but your shoulders must be relaxed and not elevated. If you are accustomed to quilting with a frame or hoop on your lap with your legs cramped up underneath you, you may already have discovered that this position does not allow you the hours of pleasure you had hoped for. If you use a pillow to support your arms or find a chair with armrests, you can hold your neck in a more comfortable position. The best solution if you cannot support your arms is to make sure you change your sitting position frequently.

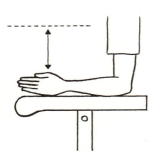

Your work should be 0 to 15 cm (0–6 in) above your elbow.

Tips on Combining Your Chair and Work Surface

Whether you are sitting at a sewing machine or quilting by hand, remember that you should not be bending your head and neck forward by more than 15 degrees or fatigue will set in and your neck will begin to hurt. You will find that by adjusting the angle of your sewing machine or quilting frame or hoop, you can improve the posture of your head and neck, significantly reducing the amount of discomfort you experience while sewing. Have someone take a picture of your posture while you are working to see the position of your body. If your back is rounded and your head and chin protrude forward, consider making adjustments to your chair and work surface.

Troubleshooting Chart for Height of Work Surface

Situation	What Happens?	Leads To	Possible Correction
1 Work surface too high	• prevents use of proper lumbar support • overstretches spine • stresses shoulders • tires whole body	• back pain • shoulder and neck pain	• raise chair (if sufficient clearance for thighs) and provide support for feet • lower work surface
2 Work surface too low	• causes you to lean forward	• slumped posture • back pain	• raise table on blocks so it is at waist level when you are standing • height of table when sitting depends on your activity (see text)

Quilting has been the centre of my social life since I moved to this city. In my current state of semi-unemployment, it's been important to have a group I feel a part of.

Catherine Rostron

6

Standing Can Be a Pain

Prolonged standing can be as stressful for your body as prolonged sitting. Since the human body is made for movement, standing still is not an easy posture to maintain without muscle fatigue. The back and legs are usually the areas of greatest complaint. Bending the head and neck forward causes additional stress and can also lead to neck and back complaints. As in sitting, it is important to move around and change positions frequently when standing. Try walking, stretching, or alternating standing with supported sitting.

In the ideal standing posture, if you were to draw a line from the ear to the foot the line would also pass through the shoulder, hip, knee, and ankle. Gravity causes our bodies to become more flexed over time, and this flexing is particularly noticeable in the upper spine between the shoulder blades. Aging and a sedentary lifestyle lead

Effects of gravity.

to the common standing posture of a protruding chin, a rounded upper back, and a protruding abdomen.

How to Stand Correctly

First you need to become aware of your body and feel the relationship between the different parts. You can take advantage of waiting time in line-ups at the supermarket or bank to work on this exercise. Practise the position until it feels comfortable.

Place your feet about 10 cm (4 in) apart with your toes pointing straight ahead and your feet parallel. Your knees should be slightly bent. Position the pelvis by tightening your buttock muscles. If you have a sway back, you will notice that it becomes much flatter with this exercise. If you have a flat back, allow the front of your pelvis to tilt forward. Place hands on your hips to feel the movement of the pelvis.

With your pelvis tilted slightly forward, focus on your abdominal muscles and tighten them so that the pelvis is held against gravity and supported in the proper position. The contents of your abdominal cavity will now be resting on your pelvic floor, where they should be, instead of against the abdominal wall. If you stand in this position, you will find your stomach does not stick out as much.

The next step is to gently tighten the muscles between your shoulder

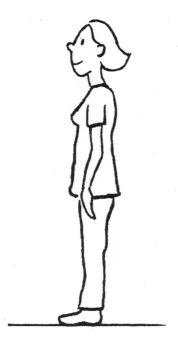

Ideal standing posture.

blades. Tightening these muscles raises the chest. Don't use your arms and shoulders to accomplish this but concentrate instead on the muscles in your upper back. Now imagine someone is pulling your head up by a strand of your hair. Your head will lift up. As this happens, gently tuck your chin in and think of making the back of your neck long. Then lean forward until you feel some pressure on the balls of your feet.

Concentrate on how this position feels. Relax. Make sure you really let everything go. Now start again. Soon you will feel what good standing posture feels like and standing correctly will begin to come naturally.

Making the Most of Standing

As a general rule, standing should always be alternated with sitting and walking to prevent your muscles from becoming fatigued in any one position. If you are standing to work on a project, you can make yourself more comfortable by correcting your standing posture frequently. You can also make standing a little easier by using a pedestal stool so that you can alternate between standing and sitting. Any activity where static standing is required—such as ironing—should be set up so that you can rest your foot on a small footrest. Alternating with one foot up and then the other will help you keep your back straight.

An article in a recent quilting magazine suggested hanging your quilt on a line to baste it. The idea is novel and has much to recommend it as it avoids the bent-over postures you need to assume when basting a quilt on a table. (Basting on the floor is worse still and very hard on the knees.)

When you stand to work, it is important to consider the height at which you have to hold your arms. The higher you hold your arms, the more unstable your body becomes and the more exhausting it is for the muscles in your back to hold your body upright.

54 Standing Can Be a Pain

When you are standing for a long time, change position frequently by raising first one foot and then the other.

Holding your arms up too high to work can lead to significant back and upper shoulder pain.

When you stand to baste a quilt, make sure the quilt is at an angle and about 0 to 15 cm (0–6 in) higher than the point of your elbow when your arm is bent at a 90-degree angle—about the level of your belt. Try to keep changing your standing position and take regular breaks to walk around or do something different for five minutes or so to alleviate the strain of standing still.

When you make a quilt and give it away, it's not yours any more but you still feel connected to it!

Catherine Rostron

Work Table Height When Standing

Quilters often spend many hours at the work surface to cut out a project with a rotary cutter. This can be very uncomfortable, not only for the legs and back, but also for the neck and shoulders. As it takes considerable concentration to avoid mistakes and accidents, there is also an element of tension!

Often the home sewing table is the same as the cutting table. The problem is, when you stand to cut, the cutting table needs to be much higher than the sewing table. Your cutting table should be waist height or slightly lower so you can avoid the sustained leaning forward postures that can cause considerable fatigue and pain.

Ideally, you should have one surface for cutting and another

Your cutting table should be at waist height.

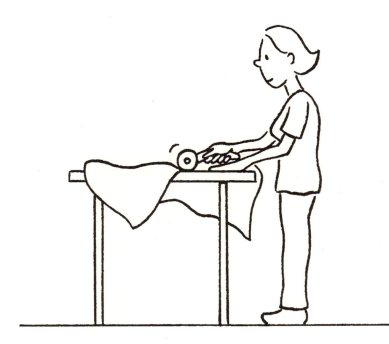

for sewing. If this is not possible, it is best to have one surface at cutting height. When you sew at this surface, you will need to mount your chair on a platform and use a footrest to support your feet.

The ironing board also needs to be adjusted so you do not have to lean over when using it. If you spend a lot of time ironing, try alternating between standing and sitting on a pedestal stool pulled up close to the board. The ideal way to manage a large ironing task is to work on it for about an hour—taking frequent short breaks to stretch—and to then move to another task before returning to the ironing.

Shoes

Whether you are standing or sitting to work on your quilting project, flat-soled footwear is best. When you are sitting down, a raised heel on a shoe tends to shorten the muscle at the back of your heel, which means you cannot rest your foot in a neutral position on the floor or on a footrest. When you are standing, a raised heel on a shoe tilts the whole body forward and you have to adjust the rest of your body to stay upright. These adjustments frequently lead to poor posture. It is difficult enough to maintain a good standing posture without the added challenge of compensating for heels on your shoes!

I love the stories of quilts—especially those quilts that relate to family and hospitality and warmth, like the log cabin and pineapple quilt. I like to write the story on the back of my quilts.

Marg Cloake

Tips on Standing Comfortably

- Wear flat-soled shoes.
- Make sure your work surface is the correct height.
- Position your work directly in front of you.
- Avoid leaning forward to reach your work.
- Alternate standing with sitting on a pedestal stool pulled up close to your work.
- Use a footrest to support one foot and then the other.
- Take frequent breaks to move around and stretch.

My mother made a scrap quilt that is now very worn but I'll never get rid of it. When you are a quilter and someone gives you a quilt, you realize that a big part of themselves has been given to you.

Barb Dawson

7

Designing Your Work Station

Many books display wonderful sewing room set-ups. For your health and comfort, each set-up should be evaluated carefully with the following principles in mind.

Organizing Your Space

Avoid Excessive Reaches
Keep equipment and objects you use frequently directly in front of, or near you. If you keep your iron to one side of your sewing machine, you need to twist your body or reach over to one side to use it. A better arrangement would be to have a swivel chair with the iron on a small table at a 90-degree angle to the work table. Now by turning the chair 90 degrees you can face the ironing surface straight on. A better option would be to place the iron and ironing board away from the sewing table so you have to get up and stretch to use them.

Although you can cut material when you are sitting down, the extended reach required for larger projects will be excessive and very tiring. It is better to stand to cut material.

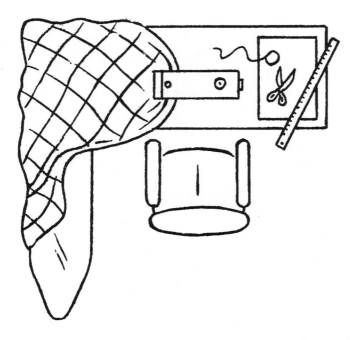

Supporting excess fabric.

- - - - - - - - -

Allow Sufficient Leg Room

The work surface must extend at least 40 cm (15–16 in) beyond your knees when you are sitting in your chair so you can sit close to your work without having to bend your body forward. You should also have room to stretch your legs once in a while when you are sitting for long periods.

Extend Your Work Surface

It is a good idea to have a sewing table extension or a separate table beside the machine to support excess fabric so that you are not attempting to hold up the project as well as guide it through the sewing machine. Supporting excess fabric places unnecessary strain on your shoulders and neck. If you do not have an extension, you may be able to move your sewing machine to free up a larger portion of the work surface to support the weight of the fabric. With a large quilt, it is helpful to place an ironing board or separate table at a 90-degree angle to the sewing machine to support the extra weight.

Lighting

Optimal lighting produces a comfortable working atmosphere. In a poorly lit area, you often need to assume an awkward position to see your work. Good lighting should make it easier to see and should distribute light evenly without producing glare or shadow. Good lighting is especially important as you age. As the lens in your eye

Good general illumination and direct task lighting.

62   Designing Your Work Station

loses its ability to focus on fine detail, you need more light to see your work. You also need more light if the contrast in the work is poor or if you have limited vision.

The immediate work area should be brighter than the surrounding areas. Natural light is best but is not always an option. If you need extra light, it is best to use adjustable lighting that you can direct to the task at hand. As well, there should be good general illumination to avoid creating too much contrast. Light-coloured walls and ceilings reflect light and enhance the general level of lighting. Clean ceilings, walls, and light fixtures also help. (As housework is usually a task that is not compatible with quilting, this suggestion may not be acceptable!)

———————————————

Housework is not compatible with quilting?

If you use fluorescent lights, make sure they are positioned properly to avoid glare, and use a grid or panel to diffuse the light evenly. You can avoid any detectable flicker by connecting the tubes to the grid so they alternate out of phase. Replace the bulbs on a regular basis.

For people with visual limitations there are products that provide magnification with local lighting. When positioned properly to optimize good sitting posture, this type of product can be a valuable tool for the quilter.

To avoid eye strain when working on a project that requires considerable concentration and close focus, periodically change your focal distance by looking farther away. This action could coincide with a postural stretch or change of position!

Organizing the Sequence of Your Work

Besides planning the set-up of your sewing centre, it is also a good idea to organize your work so that you alternate frequently between sitting down and getting up and moving around. If you need to sit for a long time—for instance, to sew a large number of strips together—make a point of getting up every fifteen minutes or so to press the fabric instead of doing the pressing all at once at the end. This method may take longer, but it provides a better balance between activity and inactivity and will result in less discomfort from sitting and straining your muscles for too long.

Some sewing room arrangements have an iron and board right beside the machine so that a turn in the chair is all that is required to reach them. Although this is an economical way to complete a task, it does mean that you then have to make a conscious effort to get up on a regular basis to move and stretch.

Sitting positions and habits vary from individual to individual. Whatever your preferences, be sure to change position regularly throughout your sewing session. By varying the angle of hips, knees, ankles, and elbows, every person can find a comfortable position.

Tips on Organizing Your Work

- Vary your tasks. For example, alternate sewing with getting up to press something.
- Try alternating chairs or using a Balans chair for a short period. (These chairs are useful for occasional sitting but they can be very uncomfortable for people who have arthritic knees or shins. Balans and other kneeling-type chairs do not support the lower back so the loading on the spine is similar to regular standing.)
- Take frequent breaks to stretch throughout your sewing session.

Balans chair.

8

Choosing Your Tools

Well-designed tools do not force joints into unnatural positions. Sometimes you can adapt a tool that is poorly designed or use it in a different way. It goes without saying that it is essential to keep your sewing tools in good working order; changing blades and regular oiling will make them more efficient.

It is not possible to review all the equipment that is available for quilters from an ergonomic point of view. The rotary cutter, however, is worthy of mention. This amazing tool has revolutionized quilting because it is accurate and easy to use. Unfortunately, rotary cutters with a wheel at the end of the handle are awkward to hold if you follow the manufacturer's directions, which indicate that your index finger should be on the top of the handle. In this position the

Preshaped hand grips are suitable for the "average" hand.

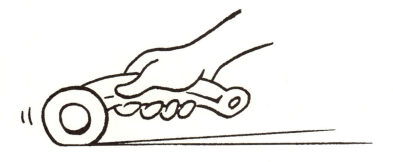

wrist is turned outwards. Whenever your hand is bent downwards or turned to either side, your grip is weakened and you cannot control the tool as efficiently as when your wrist is straight. In a constrained posture, more force is required through the joint to do the task. Increased force combined with repetitive use of the tool does not allow enough time for the muscle to recover, and fatigue becomes a problem. With continuous use over an extended period, a great deal of discomfort can develop in the wrist and hand.

Look for rotary cutters with curved handles because these increase the area of contact with the palm of the hand so you can grip them better. Of course, they are only of any use to you if they fit your hand. Preshaped hand grips do not allow for individual variations in finger thickness and grip width and are only useful if you have an "average hand."

If you need to do a lot of cutting, the best way to deal with poorly designed tools is to alternate cutting with an activity that requires a different position. For instance, you could try cutting for one hour; taking a break to stretch the muscles of your hands, forearms, shoulders, and upper neck; walking for five to ten minutes; sewing for one hour; stretching the muscles of your lower and upper back; and cutting for one hour.

If you have experienced previous joint problems and deformities, as found in the arthritic hand, the force that is placed through the joint is even greater. This can be a particularly hazardous situation for the quilter who is already suffering from joint pain. The position that is used with the rotary cutter (wrist turned outwards) should always be avoided.

The more stressed I am the more likely I am to start a quilt. Quilting keeps me sane.

Kelora Goethe

Tips on Choosing Tools

Always align your hands with your forearms as much as possible. If you work predominantly with your left hand, purchase equipment that is made for left-handed people.

Rotary Cutters
Select a cutter with a slightly convex handle that fits your palm. Avoid pre-formed grips if they do not match the size and shape of your hand.

Scissors
Select scissors with a comfortable grasp. Choose handles that are long enough to fit your whole hand to avoid pressure on your palms.

Irons
Choose an iron that is lightweight and easy to lift. If you iron a lot, check that the handle of the iron allows you to align your wrist with your forearm. For left-handed people, some irons are adapted to have the cord on one side or the other.

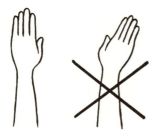

Align hand with forearm.

Time doesn't matter. I am more willing for things to take time—they don't have to be done tomorrow. If a project takes two years or more, that's okay. It's part of my maturation process, I guess.

Linda Landine

9

Other Health Hazards

Circulatory Problems

Quilters spend a lot of time sitting down. When you stand or walk, the muscles in your legs contract and relax, enhancing the circulation in your lower legs. When you sit down, the muscles in your calves relax. Without the muscle pump action in the calves, blood tends to pool in the lower legs, causing swelling and discomfort. If you already suffer from poor circulation, prolonged sitting can exacerbate this condition.

The problem is compounded if the chair you are sitting in has a firm edge that presses into the backs of your thighs. This will further inhibit blood flow to your legs and lead to even more discomfort. In people predisposed to clotting disorders, prolonged passive sitting is also considered a factor in the development of blood clots in the legs. Similarly, if you already have problems with varicose veins, swelling, or skin ulcers in the lower legs, sitting for a long

---

Quilting is a creative outlet for me. I get immense satisfaction from the process —especially the completion.

Catherine Rostron

time only makes the situation worse.

The good news is that if you are aware of the problem and take steps to counteract it, circulatory problems should not interfere with your quilting pleasure. Taking time out every half an hour or so to exercise your feet and ankles as illustrated in chapter 11 promotes good circulation. It is even better if you can get up and move around on a regular basis. Walking around continuously for five minutes out of every hour activates the muscle pump action of the calves. You can also stand behind your chair and use it for balance as you stand up on your toes. Standing on your heels and raising your toes off the floor provides a nice stretch for the back of the leg.

Setting up the sewing area to encourage a change of position is also of great benefit for the legs, as well as for the neck and back. Try organizing tasks (for example, sewing and pressing) to be done in such a way as to encourage frequent ups and downs.

Repetitive Strain Injuries

Quilting is full of repetitive tasks that if performed over an extended period with a certain amount of force may produce injury. Overuse syndrome, soft tissue disorder, tendonitis, tennis elbow, tenosynovitis, carpal tunnel syndrome, and de Quervains disease describe a range of conditions that are characterized by discomfort or persistent pain in muscles, tendons, and other soft tissues. These problems are usually chronic and long term. The main cause of all these conditions is movement that is repeated frequently in sustained and awkward postures. Forceful movements and stress can also contribute to the problem.

If you are an avid quilter, repetitive strain injuries can severely limit your ability to work on all stages of the quilt-making process. For quilters who already have signs of arthritis in their arms and hands, some quilting activities can further deform joints if preventative action is not taken. Problems do not usually arise with the first quilting project but for those quilters who are prolific over many

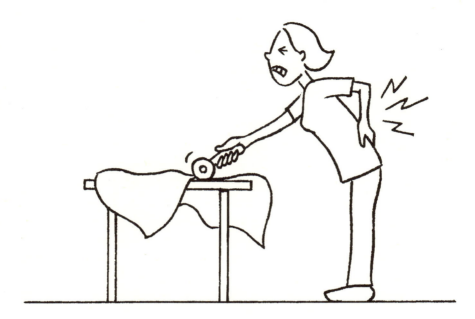

When organizing your quilting tasks, it is important to look at the whole picture.

---

years problems may arise. In the quilt-making process, there are two main culprits: hand quilting and rotary cutting. Both activities usually involve a fixed posture of the neck and shoulder and require some force.

In order to prevent repetitive strain injuries, it is important to look at the whole picture. Obtaining a rotary cutter that is designed for your hand, for example, will not be helpful if your standing posture is adversely affected by the height of your work table.

How Do Repetitive Strain Injuries Occur?

In industry there are many reports of repetitive strain injuries, especially in workers who sit at video display terminals and who work in garment manufacturing. Rates for this type of injury are rising and are expected to rise further, particularly in the communication and information fields. There are no figures for quilters; however, whenever I ask questions about musculoskeletal problems at quilt shops or listen to stories at the local guild, the information I hear suggests that the numbers are significant. What could be worse than not to be able to do what you absolutely love doing in your leisure time!

Repetitive strain injuries do not occur after one day of quilting; they gradually develop with repeated trauma over an extended period. An injury that is caused by excessive stretching or use of muscles or tendons when doing an activity for the first time may produce discomfort that lasts for a few days. If the injury is repeated on a regular basis over time, however, there will be swelling in the muscle that could lead to long-lasting disability.

It takes energy to contract a muscle. Byproducts of this expenditure of energy are removed as the blood circulates. If a muscle contraction lasts a long time (for example, when poor sitting posture at the sewing machine affects the muscles in the neck and upper back), less blood flows to the muscles. Byproducts that accumulate are difficult to remove and irritate the muscles, causing pain. The amount and type of pain depends on how long the contraction lasts and the length of time between contractions.

I had tennis elbow that started with carrying books. Quilting can easily aggravate it. Sometimes I get shoulder problems with machine quilting—maybe it's the way I'm sitting. The floor frame works well for me.

Barb Dawson

Where Does the Injury Occur?

Tendons are continuous with the fibres at the end of muscles and attach to the bones. Some tendons, mainly those in the wrist and hand, are encased in a sheath that acts like a lubricated glove. Others, found around the shoulder, elbow, and forearm, do not have a sheath.

When the muscles in the hand and wrist contract—for instance, to cause the fingers to bend—a lubricating fluid in the tendon sheath allows the tendon to slip smoothly. With repeated motion the lubricating fluid may become less efficient, and friction between the sheath and the tendon causes swelling. If the activity continues, microscopic tears appear in the tendon. The mechanical stress on the muscles and tendons is heightened if the joint is not in a neutral position. For example, if the wrist and fingers are both bent, there is more stress than if just the wrist is bent. With repeated episodes of swelling and microscopic tearing, the tendon thickens, and it is then more difficult for the joint to move.

When a tendon sheath swells, it is called a tenosynovitis. Tendons without sheaths also swell and thicken, a condition known as tendonitis. Around the shoulder, the tendons pass through a narrow space between the bones where a bursa, or fluid-filled sac, acts as a cushion between the tendon and the bone. With repeated trauma to the tendon, the bursa becomes inflamed—a condition known as bursitis.

Nerves are surrounded by muscles, tendons, and ligaments. With repetitive motions and awkward postures, the tissue around the nerves can become stretched and swollen, which puts pressure on the nerves. When a nerve is compressed, the related muscle does not work as well and becomes weak. You may also notice numbness, pins and needles, reduced circulation, and dry skin.

Recognising Repetitive Strain Injuries

Pain is the most common symptom of repetitive strain injury but stiffness of the joints, muscle tightness, and redness and swelling of the affected area may also occur. There are three stages to this type of injury. Frequently, however, the progression of the stages is not clear-cut and they can vary from individual to individual.

Early Stage

Your arm aches and feels tired when you are quilting but feels fine when you are not. You are still able to perform the activity.
- Apply cold in the form of a commercial ice pack, ice cubes wrapped in a plastic bag, or a bag of frozen peas. (Ice reduces pain and swelling.)
- Check your posture and work station set-up.
- Stretch and exercise before and while you work. If the exercises aggravate the condition, consult a physical therapist, occupational therapist, or your doctor.
- Take frequent breaks.
- Use ergonomically designed tools that fit you well.

There are a number of resting wrist and hand splints on the market. They may help reduce aches and pains but be aware that if you restrict the movement of one joint, the surrounding joints may have to work in unnatural positions, leading to other problems. Checking the basics of posture, limiting the activity, and doing stretches and exercises are better ways to get to the source of the problem. As hand shape and size vary considerably from individual to individual, in cases where a resting splint is recommended, it is best to get a trained occupational therapist, or in some places an orthotist, to custom-make a splint for you.

Intermediate Stage

You notice aching and tiredness fairly soon after you start to quilt and the discomfort lasts into the night. Now you are unable to spend as much time quilting as you would like. Treat the condition as you would in the early stage and consult a physical therapist, occupational therapist, or your doctor.

Late Stage

Aching, fatigue, and weakness persist even when you are not quilting and make it difficult for you to sleep. At this stage, you will no longer be able to spend time quilting and you should consult a physical therapist, occupational therapist, or your doctor.

The first pain you experience is a signal that the muscles and tendons need to rest and recover. This is the time to prevent further injury by correcting your posture, customizing your work set-up, and exercising regularly. If the pain persists it is time to consult your physical therapist, occupational therapist, or doctor, who have access to specialized tests to determine the extent of muscle or nerve damage.

I used to have a lot of back pain when I worked on a floor frame. Now I sit at the kitchen table with a hoop and it isn't a problem because I am sitting more erect.

Grace Whittington

Tips on Preventing Repetitive Strain Injuries

Prevention is important because medical treatments are unlikely to be effective once these injuries become long-standing.

- Stretch and warm-up the small muscles in your hand, wrist, and elbow before you start work. (See chapter 11.) The level of skill and effort that is demanded of these small muscles is an Olympian event! If you were going to run the 100-metre dash, wouldn't you get ready?
- Check your posture. You need good support for prolonged sitting, and good posture and a work surface that is the right height for standing activities.
- Balance activities. Do one thing for an hour, then take a break to do something different for the next half hour before returning to the first activity.
- Stretch every forty-five minutes.
- Relax! Tension only makes things worse.

10

Going to a Quilting Workshop

What could be more fun than spending a half day, a whole day, or a weekend with fellow quilters learning a new technique or working on a project without any interruptions! The dream day, however, frequently ends with you feeling as though you have been run over by a truck!

Aching necks and backs are the most common complaints. Trading an upper back or neck massage for some of your fabric stash should be a serious consideration. Some workshops have even considered having a massage therapist on site. Formal and informal agreements to "massage your neck if you'll massage mine" are part of some classes.

The problems in most workshops are the chairs (which are usually lousy), work table heights (unadjustable and made for the "average"), and hours spent in poor postures that lead to the lament of "I hurt all over." Then there is the added stress of carrying awkward and heavy loads with poor body mechanics.

With the knowledge that has been acquired in previous chapters, it is possible to improvise, and it is well worth taking a few minutes at the beginning of the workshop to make yourself as comfortable as possible.

Creative Comfort at the Workshop

Chair
The best solution, although probably impractical in many situations, is to bring your own customized chair from home. The next best thing is to bring a chair insert such as an Obus Forme® or a Nada-Chair® that will provide the lumbar support that is required for prolonged sitting. Alternatively, you could use a lumbar roll with a piece of Velcro sewn to the ends so it can be adjusted to fit around any size of chair. A rolled-up towel can be placed at belt level in any chair. Even a rolled-up jacket or sweater can do in a pinch.

If the workshop has a lecture format, be sure your chair is positioned so you directly face the speaker. This may require some adjustment to the seating plan, but is well worth saving your neck from an awkward, unnatural posture.

Footrest
You can use books, binders, or a portable footrest to elevate your feet and provide a better position for your back.

I made a baby quilt for friends who were moving to Texas. The pattern was bluebonnets to reflect the flowers from that state. The spring of each year they lived in Texas, the parents took a picture of their child and that quilt in a field of bluebonnets to show me how he is growing.

Catherine Rostron

Sewing Machine

If the work table is too low, put a binder or book underneath to raise it up. You can also put something under the back of your sewing machine to tilt it towards you.

Once you understand the basics of chair height and angle to table height and angle, as well as the importance of posture, you can make yourself quite comfortable.

The most important thing you can do at a workshop is to take frequent breaks to change your position and to do exercises to stretch fatigued muscles. The total environment at a workshop setting is more difficult to adjust to your individual preferences, so it is imperative to maintain good positioning. This is an enormous challenge when the subject is fascinating and you are totally engrossed in something much more interesting than your posture! Walking around to admire the work of others is a natural and pleasant way to change position. Take the time to do a few back and neck stretches whenever possible.

If you are a workshop teacher, incorporate an exercise routine or stretching break into your presentation to assist the comfort and concentration of the students. Exercising as a group frequently provides the motivation to move that most people need. Students who are comfortable are more capable of learning.

Getting to and from the Workshop

The Journey

Driving a long distance to or from a workshop with several people in the vehicle can be uncomfortable for the passenger in the front. If you have to turn your head constantly to the left to visit with the passengers in the back seat, eventually your neck will begin to hurt. Avoid this position or rotate places in the vehicle.

It is also important for the driver to practise good neck and back positions. Car seats are often poorly designed and require the addition of a lumbar roll of some kind. Driving with your chin thrust forward and your arms up for a long time can tighten and tire the muscles in your upper neck. If traffic is heavy or the drive has been difficult, there is an element of tension and stress that compounds the problem. This is definitely not a great way either to arrive at or to return home from the workshop.

Going to the workshop.

Moving Your Equipment

Transporting your equipment to and from the workshop sometimes makes it feel like moving day. Many veteran workshoppers have invested in lightweight sewing machines to ease the burden to be carried. This is highly recommended but not always in the budget.

Another approach is to find some kind of a cart. The ideal carrying device is high enough that you do not have to lift a heavy sewing machine very far up or down but can slide it from one surface to another. Move the cart by pushing it straight ahead of you with

An ideal carrying device.

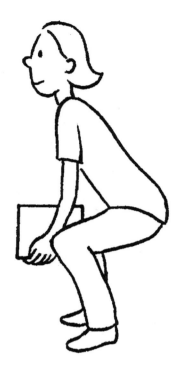

The proper way to lift heavy loads.

---

both hands on the handle. If you pull it behind you, you may find yourself having to twist your body. Avoid carts with low handles that cause you to bend forward.

If you can pull a suitcase come-along without having to twist your spine, it can be very useful. It is best to extend the handle and pull it directly behind you. Alternate pulling with the right arm and then the left arm to balance the effort on each side.

Any type of carting device (except one that causes you to lean forward to push it) is preferable to carrying heavy objects in an unbalanced fashion. Sometimes, however, you may have no choice. In these cases it is important to use the best body mechanics possible to protect your neck, back, and shoulders from injury.

When my father was in the hospital for heart surgery, I worked on a quilt to help the hours pass. It was a very emotional time for me, and the quilt became a significant part of our relationship during that time.

Kelora Goethe

Tips on Lifting Heavy Loads

- Lift with your legs not your back. Bend your knees keeping your back straight. Check the position of your back and neck before lifting, making sure the natural lumbar curve is maintained. Lift the load by straightening your knees; lean slightly backwards to stay balanced. Tighten the muscles in your abdomen and lower back before lifting.
- Keep objects close to your body.
- Adopt a wide stance to increase your base of support.
- Do not twist as you lift. Move your feet if you need to turn.
- If possible, balance your load so that it is the same on both sides. A backpack is a good solution here. (Perhaps there is a pattern out there for a quilter's tote that can be adapted with some shoulder straps to make it into a backpack?)
- It is often better to take a number of trips with smaller loads than one trip with a large load.

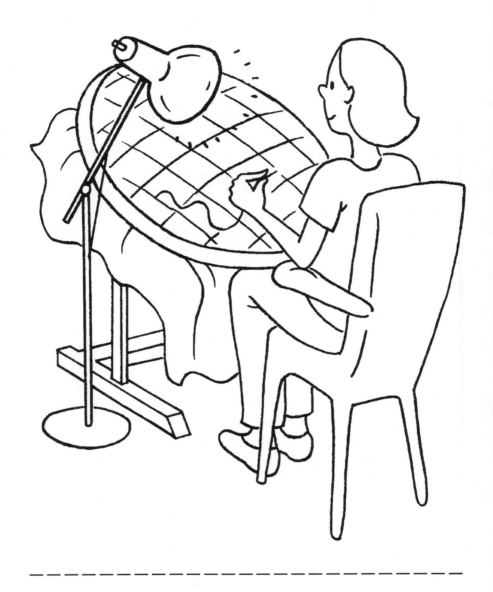

I had tendonitis in my left elbow, which I think was a combination of tennis and quilting. I gave up tennis!

Linda Landine

11

Exercises and Stretches to Make You Feel Great

When to Exercise

Back
If you have been sitting or standing bent forward for over an hour, do these exercises to minimize the risk of overstretching ligaments and other soft tissues. If you have back problems, you may find these exercises uncomfortable at first. Try them gently for a few days. If you experience more pain than usual, stop doing them and consult your physical therapist, occupational therapist, or doctor. Women over forty should do back extension exercises to reduce the effects of osteoporosis on the spine and to counteract the spine's tendency to become more flexed with age.

Neck
It is not a good idea for people over sixty to tilt their heads backwards, particularly if they experience dizziness or lightheadedness. A good chin tuck is very beneficial and adequate. Exercise your neck when you have been sitting or standing for up to an hour.

Legs

If you are predisposed to circulatory problems and you are doing a task that requires you to sit for long periods, you may need to do the exercises every forty-five minutes in order to promote circulation.

General

Everyone likes to exercise differently, but if you swim or walk continuously for at least twenty minutes a day, you will find you have more energy to enjoy the things you love to do and your general sense of well-being will be enhanced. As we get older it is even more important to incorporate general exercise into the daily routine. We need to work at staying strong in order to maintain good balance when we walk or stand.

Exercising can take time away from quilting, but in the long run, it will make those quilting hours even more enjoyable and comfortable. Finding an activity you enjoy is critical if you are going to maintain enthusiasm and commitment over the long term. Getting started is usually the most difficult part.

How to Exercise

The following exercises are organized by starting position. The ones that are described from a sitting or standing position should be easy to incorporate into your regular quilting activity. Those that must be done from a lying position on the floor will not be as easy to do when you are in the workshop setting but should be possible in your home. The stretching in the exercises should be increased gradually and should be sufficient to cause mild discomfort but not pain. Start and finish stretching *slowly*.

The Exercises

Starting position.

— — — — — —

Exercise.

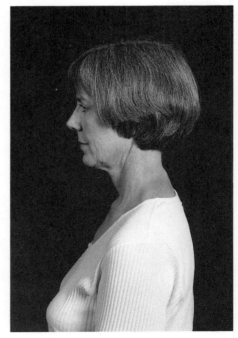

Sitting

Chin tuck—stretching and postural exercise

Sit on a chair and look straight ahead in a relaxed position. You will notice that your chin is probably poking forward. Gently pull your shoulder blades together to correct the posture in your upper back. Gently pull your chin down and back towards your neck. As you do this you may experience a double chin and a slight stretching in the back of your neck. Hold this position for a few seconds. Relax. Let your chin poke forward again and repeat the exercise. Repeat the exercise five to ten times if you are taking a break. During sewing or quilting activities, build the exercise into your work. After sewing one strip or quilting one block, use this exercise to correct your posture.

When I am quilting for a long time on a heavy quilt, I get a kink in my side which can be very uncomfortable. I usually get up and stretch and stop quilting.

Marg Cloake

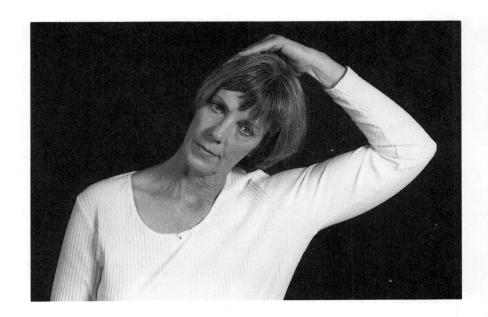

Side bend.

— — —

Sitting

Side bends

Start from a chin tuck position as described above. Bend your neck to the side keeping the chin tuck position. Gently pull your head a little farther with your hand. Hold the position for a few seconds and then repeat the exercise to the opposite side.

> **Tip**
>
> These exercises should be done whenever you take a break, but they can also be done during your sewing or quilting activities when there is a natural place to pause—for example, after completing the next strip, cutting the first fabric, and so on.

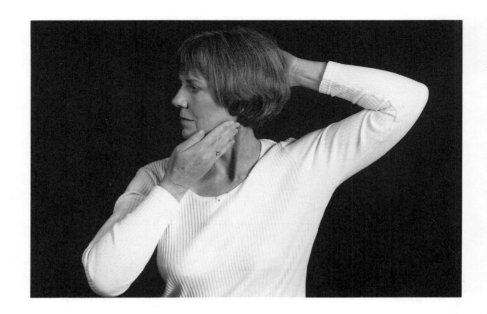

Neck rotation.

— — — — —

Sitting

Neck rotation

Start from the chin tuck position. Turn your head as far as possible to the right. Use both hands (one on your chin and the other on the back of your head) to gently but firmly help you to turn a little bit farther. Hold the position for a few seconds and then repeat to the opposite side. Be sure to start with a good chin tuck position before you turn to the opposite side.

The very worst pain I got was from lifting my sewing machine. It not only affected my shoulder but also triggered a headache. I'm also having pain in my thumb and first finger—it is probably aggravated by the work I do during the day with a microscope.

Sheilagh Basky

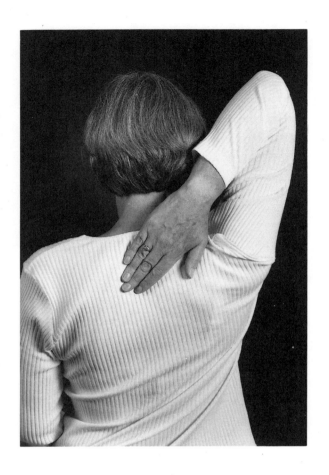

Stretching and strengthening the upper back.

Sitting

Stretching and strengthening the upper back
Start from the chin tuck position. Place your right hand on your left shoulder blade from behind your head. Reach as far as possible and then try to move your right elbow backwards. Hold this position for a few seconds. Relax. Repeat five times. Repeat with your left hand on your right shoulder blade.

The worst pain I had was while I was quilting on a floor frame. The pain between my shoulder blades moved to my chest and made me short of breath. I wondered if I was having a heart attack! I lay on the floor until it went away. I had to quit using that frame.

Linda Landine

Starting position.

— — — — — —

Exercise.

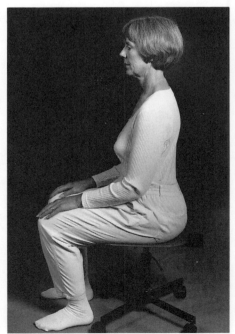

Sitting

Correcting the posture of the lower back

Sitting on your chair, slump forward with a rounded back and your arms to your sides, and then sit up with an exaggerated curve in your lower back and your hands on your knees. Hold this position for a few seconds and then repeat this exercise five times.

I used to paint but I enjoy quilting more because you can work with colour and texture. Fabric is such a flexible medium.

Shirley Collins

Stretching the middle and lower back.

Sitting

Stretching the middle and lower back

Take a deep breath in and lift your arms above your head towards the ceiling. Stretch and yawn. Lean slightly backwards in your chair to relax the muscles of your trunk and lower back. Keep your chin tucked in. Hold for ten seconds and repeat five times.

> ### *Tip*
>
> This last exercise is frequently a very natural position to assume—especially once you become aware of screaming fatigue in your back and neck! It is important to use this position on a regular basis and not to wait until you are starting to hurt. A chair that has an inclining backrest works well. If the chair comes to the middle of your back and is strong enough, try leaning backwards using the back of the chair as a pivot point. If your chair is rigid, use a footrest to change the position of your lower back in relation to your spine for fifteen to twenty minutes.

Improving circulation in the feet and ankles.

— — — — — —

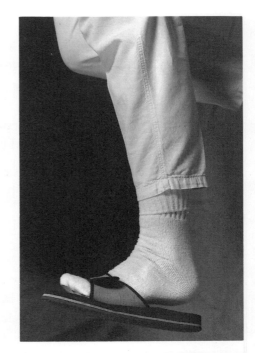

Sitting

Improving circulation in the feet and ankles

Straighten one leg out in front of you and hold. The knee should be completely straight and you should feel a slight stretching behind your knee. Holding your leg in this position, point your toes up and down five times each way (pull up and down as far as your ankle can go). Relax for ten to fifteen seconds. Straighten your leg again and make a circle with your foot keeping your leg straight. Go the same direction five times. Change direction and circle five times. Relax. Repeat with the opposite leg.

> **Tip**
>
> It is not difficult to incorporate these exercises into your regular quilting activity. If you have problems with swelling ankles and legs when you sit for a long time, elevate your feet on a footrest to relieve the pressure.

Starting position.
— — — — —
Exercise.

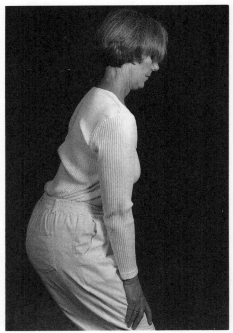

Standing

Stretching the middle back

With your knees bent and your feet about 15 cm (6 in) apart, put your hands on your thighs and support yourself in this position. Chin tuck. Lift your chest up so that you feel a stretching in your back between your shoulder blades. Hold this position for a few seconds. Relax. Repeat five times.

The sharing and comradeship of the local quilting guild is really important to me. It is a good place to share ideas—besides getting inspiration from others!

Shan Cochrane

Starting position.

— — — — —

Exercise.

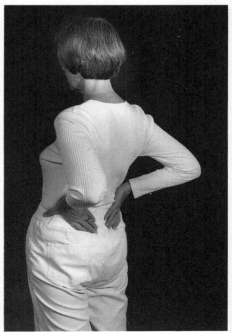

Standing

Stretching the lower back

With your feet slightly apart, place your hands in the small of your back with your fingers pointing inwards. Bend backwards from your waist using your hands as the pivot point for the movement. Keep your knees straight. Hold this position for a few seconds. Return to the starting position and repeat the exercise slowly. Each time that you do the exercise try to bend a little farther backwards. Repeat five times.

Tip

This exercise can be done easily when you stop to think about the next step in your project. If you are at a workshop and the teacher gathers everyone for a demonstration, take the opportunity to do a few back stretches!

Stretching the muscles at the front of your shoulders.

Standing

Stretching the muscles at the front of your shoulders

Stand 0.6 m (a couple of feet) away from a door frame. Place your right palm on the door frame behind you with your arm outstretched and just about at shoulder level. Turn you head to look at your hand and gently lean forward so that you feel a slight stretching across the front of your shoulder. Hold the position for a few seconds. Relax. Repeat five times on each side.

I'm always trying something new and different in quilting. Once I've finished one quilt, I want to get onto the next one—that's the challenge for me.

Shan Cochrane

Starting position (right).

— — — — — — —

Exercise (below).

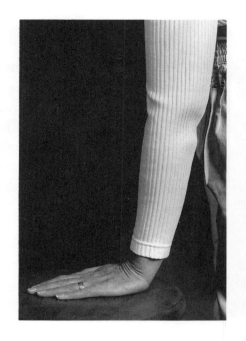

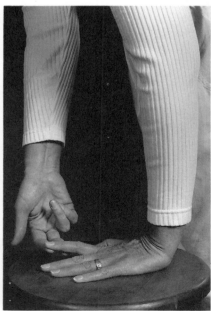

Standing

Stretching the fingers and hands

Standing at a table, place one hand palm down so that your forearm is at a 90-degree angle to your hand and your elbow is straight. Gently lean forward on your hand so that you begin to feel a stretch on the front side of your wrist and forearm. Hold the position for a few seconds. Relax and return to the starting position. Repeat five times. From the same starting position, now use the other hand to gently stretch each finger back. Do each finger five times.

> **Tip**
>
> Do stretching exercises for the hands and fingers before any activity that will require considerable effort of the muscles of the forearm, wrist, or fingers—for example, cutting with the rotary cutter for a prolonged period, quilting, and so on.

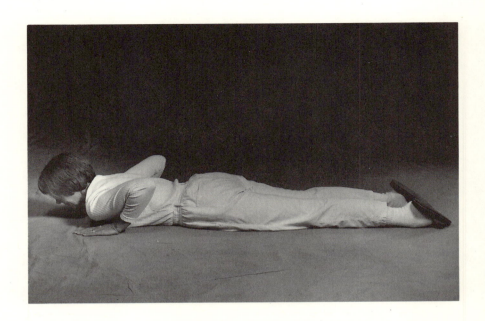

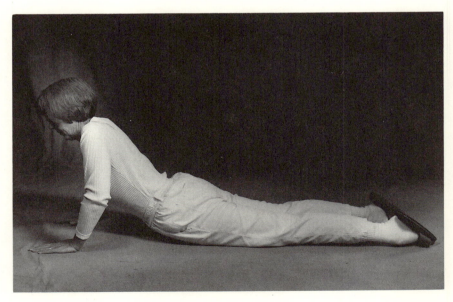

Starting position (above); *exercise* (below).

Lying

Stretching the middle and lower back

Lie on the floor on your stomach with your arms bent and your hands under your shoulders. Push the top half of your body up by straightening your elbows. Relax your lower body and pelvis while you stretch in this position. Relax and return to the starting position. Repeat the exercise five times trying to stretch your back a little farther each time.

Tip

Recent studies show that middle-aged women who regularly do back extension exercises reduce the risk of osteoporosis causing compression fractures in their vertebrae in later life. This condition affects one in four post-menopausal women and can be very painful and debilitating. Strengthening the muscles that control the posture of the spine makes it much easier for you to hold your body erect.

Exercise (above); *progression* (below).

Lying

Strengthening the lower back

Lie on the floor on your stomach with your arms by your sides. Chin tuck and then lift your chest off the floor. Hold this position for a few seconds. Relax. Repeat five times.

If you find this exercise easy, start with the same position as above but place your hands behind your neck. Lift your arms and head up to raise your chest off the floor. Hold this position for a few seconds. Relax. Repeat five times. A further progression is to stretch your arms out in front of you and then lift your arms and head up as you raise your chest off the floor. Hold for a few seconds. Relax. Repeat five times.

I have the worst pain in my neck and back when I am machine quilting. With massage therapy once or twice a week, I can keep quilting!

Betty Sanguin

Strengthening the abdominal muscles.

Lying

Strengthening the abdominal muscles

Lie on your back on the floor with your knees bent up and your feet flat on the ground. Tuck your chin in and raise your chest by reaching for your knees. It is not necessary to get to your knees, but an attempt should be made in that direction. Hold the position for a few seconds. Relax. Repeat the exercise by reaching for the outside of your right knee. Hold the position. Relax. Repeat the exercise again by reaching for the outside of your left knee. Hold and relax. Repeat the complete set of three reaches five times so that you do a total of fifteen abdominal exercises.

Quilting is a spiritual experience for me. The story of my life is wrapped up in what I create. When I start a quilt, I don't know who it belongs to. It takes on a life of its own so that when I'm finished I know who it belongs to.

Betty Sanguin

Stretching the middle and lower back.

Lying

Stretching the middle and lower back

Lie on the floor on your back with your knees bent up and your feet flat on the floor. Place your hands above your head. Rest in this position for ten minutes. It may also feel comfortable to place a small pad between your shoulder blades to gently stretch this part of the spine.

> **Tip**
>
> Lying on the floor is a good resting position but remember to be active rather than passive and do the exercises that strengthen the spine and actively stretch your back.

Quilting gives me pleasure on many levels. It is a contemplative process. I love the rhythmical repetitive nature of quilting—it's really relaxing.

                                        Shirley Collins

Equipment List

Back Supports

Canada
Ergonomic Solutions
111 Palis Way S.W.
Calgary, AB T2V 3V5
In Canada 1–800–660–3746
In the U.S. (403) 281–0880
Fax (403) 281–1690

North America
Obus Forme®
1–800–361–1378
Nada-Chair®
1–800–722–2587

Chairs

**Canada Global
Upholstery Co. Ltd.**
560 Supertest Road
Downsview, ON M3J 2M6
(416) 661–3660/
Fax (416) 661–4300

U.S.A.
Global Industries
17 West Stow Road
Marlton, NJ 08053
1–800–220–1900/
Fax (609) 596–5684

Lighting

Canada
Efston Science Inc.
3350 Dufferin Street
Toronto, ON M6A 3A4
(416) 787–4581/
Fax (416) 787–5140

U.S.A.
Edmonds Scientific
101 E. Gloucester Pike
Barrington, N.J. 08007–1380
(609) 573–6250/
Fax (609) 573–6295

North America

Spectracom Technology Corp.
1–800–WELL–LIT(935–5548)

Luggage Carts

Canada
Efston Science Inc.
3350 Dufferin Street
Toronto, ON M6A 3A4
(416) 787–4581/
Fax (416) 787–5140

U.S.A.
Jensen Tools
7815 South 46th Street
Phoenix, AZ 85044
1–800–426–1194

Portable Work Surfaces

Canada
"Adjust a Desk"
Prairie Technical
106–734 Ist Avenue North
Saskatoon, SK S7K 1Y1
In Canada 1–800–909–4405
In the U.S. (306) 244–4405
Fax (306) 244–1955

References

Bertolini, R., and A. Drewczynski. *Repetitive Motion Injuries*. Hamilton, ON: Canadian Centre for Occupational Health and Safety, 1990.

Canadian Centre for Occupational Health and Safety. *Ergonomics: A Basic Guide*. Hamilton, ON: Canadian Centre for Occupational Health and Safety, 1989.

Dul, J., and B. Weerdmeester. *Ergonomics for Beginners*. London: Taylor and Francis, 1993.

Grandjean, E. *Fitting the Task to the Man: A Textbook of Occupational Ergonomics*. London: Taylor and Francis, 1988.

McKenzie, R. *Treat Your Own Neck*. Waikanae, New Zealand: Spinal Publications, 1983.

McKenzie, R. *Treat Your Own Back*. Waikanae, New Zealand: Spinal Publications, 1985.

Nachemson, Alf L. "Lumbar mechanics as revealed by lumbar intradiscal pressure measurements." In *The Lumbar Spine and Back Pain*, pp. 162–63, ed. Malcolm I. V. Jayson. New York: Churchill Livingstone, 1992.

Panero, Julius, and Martin Zelnik. *Human Dimension and Interior Space*. New York: Whitney Library of Design, 1979.

Pheasant, S. *Ergonomics, Work, and Health*. London: Macmillan, 1991.

Stones, I. *Lighting Ergonomics*. Hamilton, ON: Canadian Centre for Occupational Health and Safety, 1989.

Zacharkow, D. *Posture: Sitting, Standing, Chair Design, and Exercise*. Springfield, IL: Charles Thomas, 1988.

Index

A

abdomen, 23, 52
   exercises for, 114–15
adapting equipment, 11, 14, 17, 27–28
   chair, 38, 40, 41, 46, 48, 49, 56, 78
   quilting frame, 47
   sewing machine, 45–46, 79
   tools, 65
   work surface, 44–49
aging, 13–14, 24, 51, 61–62, 85, 86, 111
ankles, 22, 51, 63, 70, 101
armrests, 33, 34–35, 37, 46, 47
arms, 34, 37, 43, 44, 45, 46, 47, 53–54, 71, 74, 80
arthritis, 64, 66, 71
average person, 27, 35, 47, 66, 77

B

back, 16, 20, 32, 34, 35, 40, 41, 46, 48, 53, 55, 70, 82, 83, 99, 117
   and exercise, 85
   exercises for, 94–95, 96–97, 98–99, 102–05, 110, 113, 116–17
   lower back, 19, 21, 23, 24, 32, 34, 36, 40, 64, 66, 83
   problems with, 13, 16, 19, 24, 49, 51, 54, 77
   support for, 22, 23, 24, 32–34, 36, 39, 40, 41, 64
   upper back, 13, 22, 23, 36, 43, 52, 66, 72

backpack, 3
backrest
   angle of, 32–34, 36, 39, 41
   design of, 32–34, 36
   height of, 32–34, 36, 41
Balans chair, 64
basting, 53, 54
blood clots, 22, 69
body
   measurements, 28–30
   shape and size, 27, 28–30, 31
bottom (buttocks), 23, 24, 25, 31, 32, 34, 40, 41
breasts, 32
breathing, 23
bursa, 31, 73
bursitis, 73

C

carpal tunnel syndrome, 71
cart, 81–82, 120
chair, 28–30, 31–41, 43, 63, 64, 69, 77, 78, 99
   adapting, 17, 27, 38, 40–41, 46, 49, 56
   armrests, 33, 34–35, 37, 46, 47
   backrest, 32–34, 36, 37, 39, 40–41
   buying, 35–38
   base, 33, 35
   controls, 38
   depth of seat, 32, 33, 35, 40
   dimensions of, 28–29
   height of, 32, 33, 35, 40–41, 79
   poor fit of, 22, 24, 31–32

proper fit of, 31, 32, 38
surface of seat, 31, 32, 33, 35, 40–41
swivel, 35, 59
changing positions, 24, 25, 39, 47, 51, 53, 54, 56, 57, 62, 63, 70
chin, 23, 47, 48, 52, 80
chin tuck, 23, 39, 43, 85
exercise, 88–89
circulation, 25, 72
exercise for feet and ankles, 100–01
circulatory problems, 16, 19, 21–22, 40, 69–70, 73, 86
cutting, 59, 65–67
cutting table, 55–56

D
de Quervain's disease, 71
digestive system, 16, 19, 22
discs, 19–21, 22, 24, 25
dizziness, 85
doctor, 74, 75, 85
drafting board, 44

E
elbows, 37, 39, 43, 46, 47, 54, 63, 73, 76
equipment, 11, 13, 14, 17, 28, 59
buying, 14, 27–28, 35–38
transporting, 81–82
exercises, 11, 17, 52–53, 70, 74, 75, 79, 85–117
eyes, 23, 45, 61–62

F
fatigue, 17, 22, 40, 49, 55, 74, 75
feet, 32, 35, 39, 40, 46, 49, 56, 57, 70, 83, 101
finger exercise, 108–09
fluorescent lights, 62
focal distance, 62

footrest, 34, 35, 36, 39, 40, 53, 56, 57, 78, 99, 101
forearms, 34, 37, 39, 66, 67, 73, 109

H
hand quilting, 71
hands, 16, 22, 43, 44, 45, 46, 66, 67, 71, 73, 74, 76
exercise for, 108–09
head, 22, 23, 34, 39, 43, 47, 48, 51, 79
headaches, 16
heels, 56, 70
hips, 31–32, 35, 46, 51, 63

I
ice pack, 74
injury, risk of, 13, 21, 71
internal organs, 40
iron, 59, 63, 67
ironing, 53, 56, 62–63, 64, 70
ironing board, 56, 59, 61, 63

J
joints, 14, 16, 65, 66, 71, 73, 74

K
knees, 20, 35, 40, 51, 53, 63, 64, 83

L
legs, 19, 25, 32, 40, 47, 55, 69, 83
exercises, 70, 86
problems with, 13, 21–22, 51, 101
room for, 44, 46, 60
lifting, 20, 81–83
ligaments, 19, 73, 85
lightheadedness, 85
lighting, 17, 27–28, 61–62, 119
lumbar curve, 36, 83
lumbar support, 33, 34, 36, 40, 41, 49, 78, 80
lungs, 22

lying down exercises, 20, 110–17

M
magnification products, 62
measurements (body), 28–30
measuring tape, 30
muscles, 16, 22, 32, 56, 63, 66, 69, 72, 73, 74, 75, 76, 111
    abdominal, 22, 23–24, 52, 83, 115
    fatigue in, 19, 21, 22, 24, 25, 40, 48, 51, 53, 66, 79, 80, 99
    problems with, 13, 16, 34, 71, 72

N
Nada-Chair®, 36©37, 40, 41, 78, 119
neck, 16, 19, 22, 47, 48, 55, 60, 66, 70, 71, 72, 79, 80, 82, 99
    exercises for, 85, 92–93
    position of, 34, 48, 51, 83
    problems with, 13, 24, 25, 34, 43, 48, 49, 51, 77, 79
nerves, 73, 75
noise, 17
numbness, 13, 73

O
Obus Forme®, 36, 40, 41, 78, 119
occupational therapist, 74, 75, 85
orthotist, 74
osteoporosis, 13, 85, 111
overuse syndrome, 71

P
pain, 11, 14, 16, 19, 21, 24, 25, 31, 43, 49, 54, 55, 66, 71, 72, 74, 75
pedestal stool, 53, 56, 57
pelvic floor, 52
pelvis, 32, 36
percentiles
    and body shape and size, 28–29
physical therapist, 74, 75, 85
posture, 48, 74, 75, 76, 79, 111
    exercises for, 88–89, 96–97
    good, 14, 23–24, 51–53
    poor, 13–14, 17, 21–22, 40–41, 49, 51–52, 56, 72, 77
    sitting posture, 19–25, 34, 40–41, 72, 76
    standing posture, 51–53

Q
quilting frame, 28, 47, 48
quilting hoop, 47, 48
quilting stitch, 109

R
reaching, 59
repetitive strain injuries, 71–76
respiratory system, 19, 22
rib cage, 23
rotary cutter, 55, 65–67, 71, 109

S
scissors, 67
seat (chair), 39
    depth of, 32, 33, 35, 40
    height of, 32, 33, 35, 40
    surface of, 31, 32, 33, 35, 40–41
    wedge for, 36
sewing, 64, 66, 70
    space set-up, 17, 59–61, 63, 70
    table, 45–46, 55–56, 59, 60
    tools, 65
    worksite, 28, 70
sewing machine, 45–46, 48, 59, 60–61, 63, 79, 81
    position of pedal, 46
shins, 64
shoes, 35, 56, 57
shoulder blades, 23, 34, 36, 51
shoulders, 23, 34, 37, 39, 43, 46, 47, 51, 55, 60, 66, 71, 73, 82
    exercise for, 106–07
    problems with, 24, 25, 34, 49, 54
side bends, 90–91

sitting, 14, 16, 17, 19–25, 32, 34, 37, 39, 43–49, 51, 53, 56, 57, 59, 60, 62–63, 64, 69–70, 85, 86
   exercises from sitting position, 88–101
skin ulcers, 69
soft tissue disorder, 71
spasm, 21
spine, 21, 24, 25, 32, 39, 49, 51, 64, 111, 117
   curvature of, 13–14, 51, 85
splints, 74
standing, 14, 21, 43, 49, 51–57, 59, 69, 71, 85
   exercises from standing position, 52–53, 102–09
stomach, 35, 39, 52
stretches, 11, 70, 79, 85–86, 105
stretching, 51, 56, 57, 59, 62, 63, 64, 66, 74, 76, 79, 117
swelling, 21, 22, 25, 40, 69, 72, 73, 74, 101
swimming, 86

T
tendonitis, 71, 73
tendons, 72, 73, 75
   problems with, 16, 71
   sheath over, 73
tennis elbow, 71
tenosynovitis, 71, 73

thighs, 22, 31, 32, 35, 49, 69
toes, 35, 70
tools, 62, 65–67, 74
   left-handed, 67
trunk (of body), 21, 22, 25, 32

V
varicose veins, 13, 69
vertebrae, 111

W
walking, 51, 53, 54, 66, 69, 70, 79, 86
work organization, 62–64, 70
workshops, 11, 77–86, 105
   transporting equipment to and from, 81–83
   travelling to and from, 79–80
work station design, 27, 59–64, 74, 75
work surface, 22, 27, 39, 43–49, 55–56, 76
   extending, 60–61
   for cutting, 55–56
   for designing or reading, 43–44
   for sewing machine, 45–46
   height of, 43, 45–49, 55–56, 57, 60, 71, 76, 77, 79
   slope or tilt of, 44, 45–46, 47, 79
wrists, 16, 39, 66, 67, 73, 76, 109

Author's Note

If you have read this book and enjoyed it, recommend it to others. They will learn ways they can be more comfortable when they are sitting for prolonged periods while sewing or quilting.

Consider giving this book as a gift to the quilter in your life or recommend it for use as a resource:

- by quilting teachers who wish to incorporate stretching exercises into their workshop presentations;
- for recreational quilting programs in institutions such as nursing homes;
- in your local community fitness or leisure centre library;
- in your local quilt guild library;
- at physical therapy clinics where patients are treated for the effects of prolonged sitting;
- by insurance carriers who want to promote healthy sitting and standing activities for their claimants;
- in sewing machine retail outlets where sewing machines are demonstrated;
- in quilt shops or institutions where quilting equipment is sold.

Look for *The Hidden Hazards of Quilting* by Cathy Watts in your local bookstore, or use the order form on the next page to place your order for a copy of the book.

Order Form

Canada (amounts include GST)
$24.95 per book, with a 10% discount for orders of 5 or more books, plus $3.00 shipping and handling per order. Shipping rates for more than 10 books available on request.

U.S.
US$18.95 per book, with a 10% discount for orders of 5 or more books, plus US$3.50 shipping and handling per order. Shipping rates for more than 10 books available on request.

International
US$18.95 per book, with a 10% discount for orders of 5 or more books, plus US$3.50 shipping and handling per order for airmail delivery. Shipping rates for more than 10 books available on request.

Please make your cheque or money order out to:
Physio-Diversity
1136 Temperance Street
Saskatoon, SK Canada S7N 0N8
(306) 664–3908

✂ . . . .

Please rush me _____ copies of *The Hidden Hazards of Quilting*. I understand that I may return the book for a full refund, no questions asked, if I am not completely satisfied.

Name: _____   # of books ordered _____

Address: _____

City: _____   Prov/State: _____

Postal Code/Zip: _____   Country: _____

Phone/Fax _____

Amount enclosed (books and shipping) _____